"WHEREVER A BEAUTIFUL SOUL HAS BEEN THERE IS A TRAIL OF BEAUTIFUL MEMORIES"

-- AUTHOR UNKNOWN

Remember your loved ones, share memories, write them down. Pass them on.
Books With Soul® is a trademark brand and Supports all Authors and copywrite.
Check out our full line of books amazon.com/author/bookswithsoul

Isbn: 978-1-949325-57-7

Your Words. Your Pages.

A MEMORY BOOK "REMEMBER WHEN?"

PLEASE PICK A PAGE AND WRITE A MEMORY

You taught me this...

_____
_____
_____
_____
_____
_____
_____

_____
_____
_____
_____
_____
_____
_____

I will never forget...

Remember When...

5 things I love about you...

I remember you told me...

Remember the time...

Oh this was funny...

"To LIVE IN HEARTS WE LEAVE BEHIND IS NOT TO DIE."

— THOMAS CAMPBELL

I will never forget...

Remember When...

5 things I love about you...

You make me laugh, especially when I think of this...

I remember you told me...

Remember the time...

Oh this was funny...

Remember the time...

5 things I love about you...

"WHEN YOU LOSE SOMEONE YOU LOVE,
YOU GAIN AN ANGEL YOU KNOW"

-- AUTHOR UNKNOWN

I will never forget...

You and I went here... together and I remember...

Remember When...

5 things I love about you...

You make me laugh, especially when I think of this...

I remember you told me...

Remember the time...

Oh this was funny...

Remember the time...

5 things I love about you...

"Some people come into our lives,
leave footprints on our hearts,
and we are never the same."

-- Author Unknown

I will never forget...

You and I went here... together and I remember...

Remember When...

5 things I love about you...

You make me laugh, especially when I think of this...

I remember you told me...

Remember the time...

Oh this was funny...

Remember the time...

5 things I love about you...

"DEATH LEAVES A HEARTACHE NO ONE CAN HEAL,
LOVE LEAVES A MEMORY NO ONE CAN STEAL."

-- FROM A HEADSTONE IN IRELAND

I will never forget...

Remember When...

5 things I love about you...

You make me laugh, especially when I think of this...

I remember you told me...

_____
_____
_____
_____
_____
_____
_____
_____
_____
_____
_____
_____
_____
_____
_____
_____
_____
_____
_____
_____
_____

Remember the time...

Oh this was funny...

Remember the time...

5 things I love about you...

"IT IS NOT LENGTH OF LIFE, BUT DEPTH OF
LIFE."

-- AND WHAT A GREAT LIFE

I will never forget...

Remember When...

5 things I love about you...

You make me laugh, especially when I think of this...

I remember you told me...

Remember the time...

Oh this was funny...

Remember the time...

5 things I love about you...

Those we have held in our arms, we hold in our hearts forever

— AUTHOR UNKNOWN

I will never forget...

Remember When...

5 things I love about you...

You make me laugh, especially when I think of this...

I remember you told me...

Remember the time...

Oh this was funny...

Remember the time...

5 things I love about you...

"PERHAPS THEY ARE NOT STARS IN THE
SKY,
BUT RATHER OPENINGS WHERE OUR LOVED
ONES SHINE DOWN
TO LET US KNOW THEY ARE HAPPY."

-- AUTHOR UNKNOWN

I will never forget...

Remember When...

5 things I love about you...

You make me laugh, especially when I think of this...

I remember you told me...

Remember the time...

Oh this was funny...

Remember the time...

5 things I love about you...

LIKE A BIRD SINGING IN THE RAIN,
LET GRATEFUL MEMORIES SURVIVE IN TIME
OF SORROW.

-- ROBERT LOUIS STEVENSON

I will never forget...

You and I went here... together and I remember...

Remember When...

5 things I love about you...

You make me laugh, especially when I think of this...

I remember you told me...

Remember the time...

Oh this was funny...

Remember the time...

5 things I love about you...

"FOR DEATH IS NO MORE THAN A TURNING OF US OVER FROM TIME TO ETERNITY."

-- WILLIAM PENN

I will never forget...

You and I went here... together and I remember...

Remember When...

5 things I love about you...

You make me laugh, especially when I think of this...

I remember you told me...

Remember the time...

Oh this was funny...

Remember the time...

5 things I love about you...

"IN THE END, IT'S NOT THE YEARS IN YOUR LIFE THAT COUNT. IT'S THE LIFE IN YOUR YEARS.

-- ABRAHAM LINCOLN

www.ingramcontent.com/pod-product-compliance
Lightning Source LLC
Chambersburg PA
CBHW060503240426
43661CB00007B/900